7 Relationship-Killing Mistakes With A Capricorn Man

... And How To Easily Avoid Them!

by Anna Kovach

The 7 Most Common Relationship-Killing Mistakes With A Capricorn Man... *And How To Easily Avoid Them!*

Introduction

Thank you for purchasing this copy of the *7 Most Common Relationship-Killing Mistakes... and How to Avoid them with your Capricorn Man.*

After writing the original *Capricorn Man Secrets* (https://CapricornManSecrets.com) I have had the pleasure of receiving feedback and questions from women just like you.

Women who are successful, strong, beautiful, and who have so much love to give, yet hit stumbling blocks when it comes to a relationship with a Capricorn man. The most heartbreaking thing is when a woman emails me to tell me she knows she made a mistake with her Capricorn man and asks for advice on how to fix it. Now, **many times there is some way to get back on track** and I'm always happy to offer as much insight and advice as I can.

But...

Sometimes, the critical mistake is only realized when things have gone too far. When it's too late. When she's committed one (or more) relationship-destroying mistakes without even realizing it.

As an optimistic Gemini, I still try to find ways the relationship may be salvaged. Never say never, right? Life is mysterious and miracles happen.

But when you really love your Capricorn man, *the last thing you want to do is push too far and then hope for a miracle.* It occurred to me that it would be far better to help women to avoid making these relationship-killing mistakes in the first place.

If unintentionally undermining the relationship can be avoided, that's always best. An ounce of prevention sure is worth a pound of cure. Yet mistakes do happen. We're human. So the next best thing is to know the best ways to recognize the mistake and bounce back as soon as possible.

By reading this book, you'll learn what mistakes a Capricorn man can't easily forgive. You'll know how to avoid these critical errors but also, you'll know how to get back on track in case you do fall into one of these traps in your relationship.

When you know how to not trigger these relationship-destroying issues, you'll have a much smoother connection. Life is challenging enough; your Capricorn man needs to be your ally and partner. It's best to learn how to avoid these common conflicts altogether.

What Women Assume about Capricorn Men (And why it's a mistake...)

I know you're eager to get to the good stuff; to dive right in to the common mistakes women make with a Capricorn man. But before we get down to business, as a Capricorn man would say, we have to set the framework.

Many of the common mistakes we make in any relationship with any person boil down to the same basic things. We make assumptions about each other. I know, you may think, "I don't make assumptions about anyone!"

Yet we all do this. We all have core beliefs in our subconscious that lead our decisions. On a daily basis, we size each other up in an instant. We assess each other based on our own expectations and inner rules. We project our own needs on to each other.

We all do this. It's normal. When we clash with another, it's because our core assumptions of what someone "should" do is not aligned with what they believe others "should" do.

The problem is that sometimes we forget these assumptions are just that. Since they are so core to our beliefs and decisions, we treat these assumptions as universal truths - which they aren't. When others don't live according to our standards it can be immensely frustrating.

Especially with a Capricorn man. His core assumptions seem like they're carved in stone facts because he's a concrete thinker. It takes a little extra understanding to work around this and to be flexible with him.

Here are the common assumptions women make about Capricorn men. Though I have grouped the assumptions by the element of each sun sign (air, water, fire, earth) it is wise to read each one. You may be a water sign like Pisces, for example, but have a number of important planets in fire signs. In that case it can be helpful to read both descriptions.

What other Earth Signs assume about Capricorn men

Capricorn is an earth sign. The earth signs are most likely to see their core beliefs as being universal truths. They have a hard time being flexible both in ideas and actions. They are practical, nurturing and grounded, and help others find stability.

So while earth sign women can easily understand Capricorn men, being of the same element, they may still make some core assumptions. For example, an earth sign woman will assume a Capricorn man in love with them will be generous and want to make her feel comfortable by spending lots of time together. She will also imagine they can be a great power couple, enjoying the best luxuries life has to offer.

Sometimes this is true. But very often, a Capricorn man will show his love by burying himself in work so that some day he will be able to afford all the nice things he dreams of. He does this as a means of being able to spoil his love and treat her to luxuries.

Sometimes, a Capricorn man will be much more frugal and this can leave an earth sign woman feeling he doesn't value her. Earth signs often use money or material objects to convey their love, though a Capricorn man can be thrifty. It's important for an earth sign woman to know not to personalize this. Look instead for ways he does demonstrate his love and connection.

What Air Signs assume about Capricorn men

Air signs are talkative, intelligent and flexible. They assume communication will solve all problems. They also believe that when you love someone, you'll want to talk to them a lot. You'll want to know what's on their mind. Constantly.

This is not true of a Capricorn man, though.

He doesn't have much use for small talk. He's efficient. He's intelligent but prefers to be organized and focus on his work. He may be quiet and reserved and this can confuse an air sign woman.

Yet if you are able to learn his language (it's physical, not verbal) you'll know he shows love by doing things for you rather than talking to you. You may also have to modify how you communicate.

Being too wordy can overwhelm a Capricorn man. He wants to get right to the point. He texts briefly and prefers "memos" to long and emotional emails.

What Fire Signs assume about Capricorn men

A Capricorn man will surprise fire sign women in love. Fire signs are passionate, direct and assertive. A Capricorn man can appreciate this.

Yet fire signs fight for what they want. They boldly and courageously assert their ideas and chase what they want.

Yet a Capricorn man doesn't want to be chased. He doesn't like being overwhelmed by too much direct action. He's also slow-moving.

A fire sign woman may wonder, "Why isn't he fighting for the relationship?"

She thinks in terms of fighting for what she loves. He thinks in terms of working tediously behind the scenes to set a firm foundation. He doesn't rush into anything.

What Water Signs assume about Capricorn men

Water signs tend to be emotional, empathic and nurturing. They can also be intuitive. A Capricorn man is a realist. He is not as emotionally in tune. A water sign woman can help balance a Capricorn man's personality.

Yet water sign women may feel a Capricorn man is too aloof and cold. You may see him as distant and wonder where you stand with him.

This is because he doesn't open up emotionally, even when he is in love. This can confuse water sign women. If he doesn't show sentimentality and empathy, a water sign woman will feel rejected or abandoned.

It takes some adjustment to not take his rational and practical nature as a personal rejection. Try to balance your energy with his. Understanding his practical style is the key to not feeling he is pushing you away.

1. If you Lack Self-Discipline or Disregard Rules, He'll Lose Interest

A Capricorn man is devoted to order and rules. This is easy to understand when you see that he never runs red lights and pays all his bills on time. Yet the impact of his need for discipline and routines in a relationship can be overlooked, and this can really harm the relationship.

Georgia's story:

Georgia always had a flowing, easy going personality. She struggled in school because sticking to rigid deadlines and following standardized tests and rules was difficult for her.

She preferred to find out what routines worked best for her. When she started her own business and found a satisfying niche in the gig economy, the flexibility and autonomy was perfect for her.

Though Georgia didn't follow the same structure as most of her friends with nine to five jobs, she found a way to follow her own routines. Georgia thrived when she could set her own pace. When she worked for companies that had strict, rigid rules, it felt too confining. She was glad to finally have the freedom to go at her own pace.

When she met Dylan, she felt in love almost right away. He was much slower to open up, as is true for most Capricorn men. But he admired her gumption and her willingness to pursue her passion through her business.

As their relationship developed further, Dylan would try to keep a regular schedule of when they would spend time together. He had a busy schedule during the week but had weekends free. This wasn't always the case for Georgia. Sometimes she had a Tuesday off, sometimes she worked all seven days.

Sometimes her shifts started later in the day, sometimes earlier. She tried to give him an idea of her schedule in advance so he could plan around her, but often things would come up at the last minute and she would have to cancel plans.

Dylan was getting frustrated. Georgia could understand this but was used to the flexibility. She didn't realize just how frustrating the lack of routines and schedule was to a Capricorn man.

Another point of contention was that although Georgia was on point when she was setting her work priorities, but she didn't have much self-discipline outside of her work. She would let dishes pile up in the sink. When she was not working, she preferred to be very casual. She didn't get too stressed about paying bills on time. Her attitude was, "I'll get to it eventually."

Though they had a great connection to each other, the more Dylan came to see her lackadaisical lifestyle, the more anxious and frustrated he started to become. He would try to get her to stick to a routine. He even "gifted" her with a dry erase calendar to put on the wall and list chores on.

Georgia was offended by this, thinking it reminiscent of a parent trying to get a child to do chores. They argued and he came out and told her how unsettling he found many of her habits. To Georgia, this came like a punch in the stomach. She felt like she was being picked apart. Like all the great things about their relationship were being crushed by his sudden outpouring of criticism.

What she didn't know was that it is a Capricorn man's nature to try to keep things stable. He doesn't like to complain and will stifle himself. Until he can't anymore. Then he'll pinpoint all the things he doesn't agree with or doesn't like.

Georgia, like most of us, took his words personally. Who wouldn't? But when she later did some research about Capricorn men and stepped back to think about the situation, she realized he wasn't criticizing her.

He was expressing frustration with her routines or lack thereof.

He was expressing frustration with her lack of self-discipline.

These are discrepancies that exist between different individuals whose lifestyles and preferences don't always match.

When Georgia realized how much a Capricorn man needs structure and stability, she could then empathize with his frustration. She wondered if she would be able to fit in with the rigid expectations he had.

After a few days with no contact, Dylan called her. He apologized for over-reacting and explained that he felt most comfortable with his routines, but that he didn't want her to change who she was. He told her he would try to be more accepting, but that he would feel more comfortable if there was more consistency and order in their relationship.

He had thought it out and realized that her lifestyle in her own place was out of his control. It was more their inconsistent routines together that was a source of contention.

They were able to work out their differences and Georgia tried to be mindful of keeping up with her own routines, following his example. Even when their relationship became more serious and they moved in together, they divided up tasks to play to each of their strengths. She dealt with her own bills and finances but when it came to shared expenses, he would be in charge of making sure bills were paid on time.

This gave him some relief, knowing that if Georgia was more casual with her organizational skills it wouldn't affect him directly.

A Capricorn man needs structure

Love should conquer all but the truth is that a Capricorn man needs structure and discipline. He loves to have his routines and lifestyle organized. He's got an excel spreadsheet for everything. He also needs to feel in control.

He does this by being in control of his external environment. He may love you, but he'll be turned off by a chaotic environment. If you have a haphazard approach to your lifestyle, a Capricorn man will think twice about the relationship.

If you can compromise with him and create more structure, that's great. If you can't, that's ok. Be yourself. But also try to arrange the relationship so that your lifestyles don't negatively affect each other.

If he needs to be in a tidy, neat setting and you have a lax cleaning schedule because of your other obligations, spend time at his place. If he needs every bill to be paid on time, keep your bills separate or let him be in charge of making the payments.

If he needs to know exactly what he's going to be doing several months in advance, then that can be trickier. Try to schedule set routines together that can have some flexibility in case of emergency.

Don't be too casual with a Capricorn man

Try to not be too lax with a Capricorn man. Spruce up your routines. Set an agenda for yourself. Be goal-oriented and use lists, schedules or apps to help keep yourself organized.

If you are deeply averse to such measures, as Georgia was, try your best to respect his need for orderliness and organization. Something Georgia learned over time in her relationship with her Capricorn man was that she would do much better when she came up with her own structure in her own way.

She was less likely to respond favorably when someone else set the rules for her. She needed to do things in her own style. Yet they found a way to work together.

Appreciate his hard-working nature

Sometimes a Capricorn man's insistence on organizing his sock drawer, alphabetizing his record collection by artist, or plotting out an entire year's activities all in one week can be annoying.

Yet if you flip this frustration around and show appreciation and love for his hard-working nature, you may be able to diffuse some of this frustration. Feeling gratitude instead of anxiety or frustration is always beneficial.

When you show gratitude and appreciation for his hard-working nature, you'll be able to build a stronger connection. You'll also be able to see his perspective when you focus not on the tedious aspects of his efforts but the outcome he's striving for.

2. Wasting Money will Turn off a Capricorn Man

Financial fallout is one of the most common reasons for divorce and relationship problems. Often, financial struggles come down to having different financial priorities. Remember the assumptions we looked at in the beginning of this book?

In addition to assumptions, we all also have different priorities. Some people want to live life to the fullest while others are only happy when they see a certain amount of money in the bank.

When you're in a relationship with a Capricorn man, it's important to recognize just how important financial security is to him. Remember, no matter how much he loves you, a Capricorn man will put his financial and personal security above almost everything else.

Geneva's story:

Geneva was a classic romantic at heart. She loved watching romantic movies and dreamed of the day her love interest would sweep her off her feet. But after a series of failed relationships, she was becoming convinced this would never happen.

Until she met Charles.

Charles was everything she'd dreamed of. He seemed to be very attracted to her as well. Their early courtship went smoothly. After a few months, he made it clear he was serious about their relationship and wanted to make a serious commitment.

The relationship was a dream come true.

Until they moved in together.

As is the case with many relationships, a couple doesn't really get to know each other until they actually live together. Then a whole other side of each person's personality emerges.

Now that their lifestyles were completely interconnected, Charles was taken aback by Geneva's spending habits. She would come home from a shopping trip with friends, hands filled with bags overflowing with clothes, shoes, and gifts for him and for her family.

This would make Charles bristle. He was a conservative saver who preferred to save for a rainy day rather than splurge on luxuries. She wanted to go out to eat three or four nights each week with friends. Charles took for granted that their frequent dates out were part of courtship routines. He assumed when they settled down and there was no longer a need to "impress" each other by dating and going to high-end restaurants every week, they would just enjoy a domestic relationship.

Geneva was carefree with her spending because she worked hard and felt it was important to treat herself and reward herself. She believed that material luxuries were a key to showing love and self-care.

Charles had a very different view on financial management.

They started arguing and were on the verge of breaking up when Geneva's research on Capricorn men led her to me. After a few emails back and forth, she came to understand how important financial security was to Charles.

Money means different things to different people. To Geneva, it was just a means to an end. A way to enjoy life's luxuries. To Charles, it was a means of creating long-term security.

She saw no value in saving for things that may or may not happen if there was something that could make your life better or more enjoyable now.

Charles, as a Capricorn, looked at this attitude as careless and even immature. Neither is objectively right or wrong. They just have different priorities.

After a brief break in their relationship, Geneva decided to try to slow down her spending just to see what would happen. When Charles reached back out to her, he offered her a gift. An expensive necklace. He told her he'd realized during their break that she made him happy and that as much as he wanted to be financially cautious, he also wanted to enjoy his life. With her.

They decided to give it another try.

To her surprise, Charles tried to lighten up a little and splurge here and there to show his affection for her. As much as she loved this, she didn't want to make him uncomfortable. She, too, tried to compromise and set financial goals to slow down her spending.

A Capricorn man needs to see your resourceful side

Whether you are a financial maven or not, a Capricorn man has to see that you are savvy about your resources. When something breaks, can you fix it? Are you good at keeping a budget? Can you make your favorite meals at home instead of eating out frequently? Do you know how to mend your own clothing?

He loves to see your self-sufficiency. But even if you're not on a solar-powered urban homestead growing all your own food, he will still feel reassured when he sees you are resourceful.

Though many cultures have become wasteful, seeing everything as disposable, remember this is offensive to a Capricorn man on a deep level. If he sees you casually discarding clothing that just need a simple repair, food that has been left to rot or things you could otherwise fix, he'll assume that you have an equally cavalier attitude about the relationship.

He will assume you could discard the relationship easily as well.

So when you get down to the core issue, his frugality is kind of romantic. It comes from the same desire to preserve what has value, just like his desire to hold on to the relationship and make it work even when things are challenging.

Get your finances in order

It's a good idea to get your finances in order when you get into a relationship as a means of clarifying your goals. Especially if you plan to live together, eventually marry or even have a family.

You may have a more lackadaisical style of managing finances when compared to your Capricorn man. But even if you don't match his style exactly, he'll want to see that you are cognizant of your finances.

Don't do this for him primarily; do it for yourself. Take stock of outstanding debts. Start or revise your monthly budget. Be honest with yourself about your spending habits. No need to judge yourself; just think of it like you're doing research into your financial situation.

Take some steps to know where you stand financially and where the majority of your money is going. Make long-term goals. If you're planning to get a home together, does your credit need to be repaired? If you plan to have a family together, do you need to make some adjustments to your finances in order to get ready for the added expenses of married and family life?

3. Trying to make a Capricorn man open up

Every day, I receive at least a handful of emails specifically asking about how to get a man to "open up." The answer is not always so straightforward, depending on his sign.

When you really think the language we use to describe helping a man soften up and make a commitment, we say things like, "How can I *make him open up*?" or, "He's a *tough nut to crack*!"

Ouch! It suddenly starts to sound less like romantic connection and more like conducting invasive and aggressive surgery!

Our words convey our meaning. When we try to make him open up, we're taking a proverbial crowbar and trying to break into his emotional vault.

It's no wonder so many men resist this!

Maria came to realize this after spending energy and time trying to push through the boundaries of her Capricorn love, without even realizing it.

Marla's story:

Marla was never the kind of woman to fall in love quickly. She usually took her time before getting serious. That's why it surprised her when she fell completely and passionately in love with Randy.

Her feelings for him developed much quicker than what she was used to. She knew right away he was the one for her. She felt a connection that was otherworldly. Not one to believe in soulmates, this all took her by surprise. She wasn't sure what to do or how to react.

So she did what she usually did when her heart was set on a decision. She began to pursue the relationship with intensity.

She didn't realize Capricorn men could be so cautious and distant in relationships. Not only was Randy cautious at first, but he never really opened up with the reckless abandon and intense passion she had always seen portrayed in romance movies.

When they were out on a date, he was attentive. But other than that, she felt like they were at a business dinner together rather than a romantic night out.

He was always a perfect gentleman but was so aloof. She began to panic, worrying that this amazing connection wouldn't last. Marla went online and did some research to learn more about how to get a man to open up. Unfortunately, she kept her research general. Without knowing the nuances at play in a relationship with a Capricorn man specifically, she was setting herself up for disaster.

She learned all kinds of tips and tricks and even some downright manipulative strategies to try to get to his heart. Yet without knowing how important boundaries were for a Capricorn man, one by one her tricks and strategies backfired.

She was running out of hope. Not only was he aloof to begin with, but now that her attempts to rein him in had failed, he was acting even more distantly. He could see through her attempts and was turned off.

Like any Capricorn man, Randy had a good sense of timing and was secure in knowing what was best for him. Capricorn men are very sensitive to timing. Though Marla felt very strongly that Randy was the one for her, he wasn't convinced that it was the right time to settle down.

Eventually, Marla stumbled upon my website and sent an email asking for advice.

I'll share the instructions I sent to her:

- Give yourself a week without contacting him. If he reaches out, reply, but don't initiate contact.
- In this time, spend some time doing something good for yourself each day.
- Contact a friend or family member each day for conversation.
- Take care of some business around your home you've been putting off.

What does all of this do? It's not magic. It's practical. The more energy Marla spent on herself and her own life, the less energy she was focusing on Randy. This allowed her to "breathe life" back into her own self-care and every area of her life. It sounds simple, and it was, but it was a powerful way for her to re-center herself. Capricorn men don't like to be under the microscope.

After less than a week, he responded. She didn't focus on the mistakes of the past or make any emotional confession, professing her love for him. She knew by now that this would come across as being too needy.

She continued to pay attention to her needs and nurture the relationship.

"Savor it like a meal," I had told her. "You don't want to rush through to get to the end, right?"

She followed this advice and their relationship grew stronger.

The problem Marla faced happens to a lot of us. We get so excited, so swept away by a new relationship, that we instantly assume that our love interest must also share our intense desire to get serious in the relationship.

What's more, if we become so certain of a love interest's "status" as our destined soulmate, we may actually make some serious mistakes that push him away. Whether he's a soulmate or not, he will be driven away by your attempts to get him to open up or move faster than he is comfortable with.

He'll open up in his own timing

Trust a Capricorn man's sense of timing. His planetary ruler is Saturn. Saturn is the planet of restrictions, discipline, and hard work. In Greek, Saturn is Kronos. His Greek name is the root of words like, "Chronology" or, "Synchronicity." That is because Kronos and the root "Chron" deal with timing and right timing or divine timing.

A Capricorn man has an inner clock that is aligned with the divine timing that he needs to follow in order to be successful. He's naturally like a conductor, always making sure the trains run on time.

Now, if you show up to the train station early and try to rush things or if you are running late and hoping the train schedule will be altered to fit your comfort, you may be disappointed, right?

Just like the train conductor, a Capricorn man knows there is a reason to divine timing. It's not just about the pace of a relationship being right; it's also about the pace of his entire lifestyle, including his work and many responsibilities.

Capricorn men will not change their schedules to accommodate their feelings any more than a train conductor will take special requests to alter the train's scheduled departure time.

He can teach you lessons about patience

Though it can be frustrating, a Capricorn man can teach you lessons about patience. He can help you further cultivate your own sense of divine timing. He can help you learn to let go and trust the process, rather than feeling the need to control the journey.

Give a Capricorn man the benefit of the doubt and work on learning ways to ground yourself and be patient. One of the best things you can do in a relationship with a Capricorn man is to have plenty to keep you busy. Keep in touch with friends, and nurture your interests and hobbies. Have things to do so that you aren't checking the phone waiting for his text or call.

The more responsibilities you have outside of the relationship, the more he will feel attracted to you as well. He loves it when people are involved in work and community activities. He feels a natural desire to work for the betterment of the community and to preserve stability. If you are involved in similar types of work or voluntary activities, it warms his heart.

He won't tolerate manipulation

A Capricorn man is not as intuitive as, say, a Scorpio or Cancer man. Yet he will feel the subtle push if you are being manipulative or trying to push him to move forward faster than he is comfortable with.

He won't tolerate any kind of manipulative behavior. He's straightforward and says exactly what he thinks, usually in as few words as possible. He doesn't understand why everyone else doesn't communicate in the same way.

If you try to use subtle pressure to "encourage" the relationship, he will either miss the hints altogether or become perplexed and turned off that you are trying to push him to open up or commit before he's ready.

The best thing to do is to show him that you are steady, mature, stable and responsible. Rather than trying to convince him you're the one, show him through your actions that you are the woman he dreams of. Here are a few of the **key traits he looks for in a partner:**

- Financial responsibility
- Good work ethic
- Steady employment
- Traditionalist
- Family-centered
- Minimal emotional expression
- No drama
- Slightly more nurturing than he is, but not emotionally intense

- Honest
- Loyal

He's attracted to maturity. Regardless of age, if you act like you are able to keep control of a situation and let rationality prevail over emotion, he will feel more comfortable with you.

He may act like you're a business partner rather than a romantic partner at first. He's got a low-key nature when it comes to emotion and affection. The more he feels secure, the more he will begin to ease up and show his emotional side (in small doses).

4. Causing a Scene or Being too Controversial

To a Capricorn man, reputation is everything. He doesn't want any kind of scandal or drama to impact his image. This is not for the same reason as, say, a Leo man, who is concerned with ego and appearances.

For a Capricorn man, his status and reputation are less about himself as an individual (as is the case for Leo) but about the reputation of his work or his legacy.

He's thinking of the impact his work leaves on the community for generations to come, not about whether people like or dislike him personally. Still, if you make a move that hurts his reputation or embarrasses him, a Capricorn man won't be forgiving.

Jennifer's story:

Jennifer and Neil had been dating for several months. Their relationship was becoming more serious. Neil often worked long hours, which he made clear in the beginning of the relationship was part of the "package deal" for any woman he dated. His job's demands had gotten in the way of several past relationships, and he wanted to make sure Jennifer understood that he was not always available for periods of time.

At first Jennifer was fine with this. They were just getting to know each other and she was busy as well. But after some time, the long evenings alone started to get to her. Neil was available less frequently, it seemed.

Although they were exclusive, she started to wonder if he may be seeing someone at work. She decided she would take some measures to make it known he was with her.

She called her friend, a local florist, and ordered a towering flower display complete with balloons and had it sent to him at work.

She waited to see his response when the "surprise" arrived.

Nothing.

When he texted her to check in that evening, he still didn't mention it. She was disappointed and now felt awkward and didn't want to bring it up. A week went by and it seemed he was now texting her even less.

She decided she would order his favorite meal, from his favorite restaurant and surprise him yet again at work. She figured this would make a good impression on him and also send a clear signal to whoever it was she imagined he was dealing with behind the scenes (an assumption still in her mind yet unverified by any evidence).

She showed up with a packaged three course meal. It was later in the day so she didn't expect many people would be at the office. She thought maybe she would even "catch" him with another woman, and then her suspicions would be validated.

Instead, she found an almost fully-staffed office. When she asked for him, she was told he was in a meeting. The receptionist called him out of the meeting when Jennifer showed her she had brought dinner for him.

Neil came down to the front lobby ten minutes later. He didn't look happy. He accepted her offering of dinner but didn't invite her to stay and enjoy it with him. He mumbled something that may have been "thanks." She couldn't tell exactly.

Again, this was not the reaction she had expected.

She was crushed. Though it seemed apparent now he was not up to any secret affair, she still wasn't getting the attention she wanted from him.

Just the opposite, in fact.

He dropped off with his communication significantly after that. Jennifer started to panic. She went online to research all the dating advice she could find. When nothing seemed to address her concerns, she came across my website and contacted me.

In our early conversations, I described the exact information I am sharing with you now. Her intentions were good. She was trying to protect her heart and also was trying to encourage the connection with her Capricorn man. Many other men would have responded favorably. Not to the suspicion, necessarily, but to her attempt to be warm and show her interest.

A Cancer, Pisces or Libra would have been flattered. Maybe even a Leo or Scorpio would too.

But to a Capricorn man, such a display is not endearing. He'll see the measure as dominating and also as interrupting him from his work. Never, ever do this. He will also see it as a grandiose measure that is not warranted.

A Capricorn man isn't trying to hide you; he just doesn't want you to be in his work business. He separates his work life from his personal life. If you show up at his office to surprise him, it feels awkward and distracting for him. He doesn't want to deal with any office gossip and would rather avoid this kind of display altogether.

It took a few weeks before he responded. He finally contacted Jennifer after she stopped texting him. In fact, she thought the relationship was over.

When he contacted her again, they resumed some light communication. It took another month before they saw each other again. In that time, Jennifer had the chance to apologize for being too forward and going overboard. Fortunately, she had a chance to continue the relationship once the air was clear.

A Capricorn man keeps a low profile

I can't emphasize enough that a Capricorn man keeps a low profile. This is critical to him. It doesn't mean he is ashamed of you. He's not hiding you. He probably doesn't have a secret lover. Capricorn men are workaholics and have no time to date behind the scenes in most cases.

It just means he likes to be private and avoid drama or gossip.

Objectively speaking, there is nothing Jennifer did that could outright harm his reputation. Yet to a reserved Capricorn man, her gesture of kindness, even if you sweep aside her ulterior motive, was unsettling to him.

A Capricorn man needs to feel like he can be part of a discreet and supportive partnership. He's usually not out to be a celebrity power couple. Leave that to a Leo guy.

Instead, he wants to keep a low profile. Any room for gossip or trouble will turn him off. It's obvious to see how certain displays of chaos and drama would be bad for any relationship, but with a Capricorn man, even things that are typically "normal" may be a bit over the top for him.

Don't tarnish his reputation

Be as protective of a Capricorn man's reputation as he is. Even in his personal life, he frequently thinks of his actions the way a business CEO thinks of their company's brand. Be cognizant of this in the way you treat him or talk about him.

Be careful to not share too much of your personal relationship information on social media or with friends without his permission. Be mindful that some things, which are no big deal to you, may be a very big deal to a Capricorn guy who is protective over his image and public status.

Take the time to get to know his boundaries. If you have no problem with him telling your business to his family, don't assume that he is equally lax about your family knowing details of his personal life, for example.

Avoid bringing him in to controversy

Take this to heart. If you are feisty and daring and don't mind facing down a conflict or getting embroiled in a controversial issue, that is great. Don't expect a Capricorn man to meet you on the front lines, though.

Whether you are involved as a community activist or just like to jump into the fray on social media to share your opinion, do what is meaningful for you but don't be surprised if your Capricorn love distances himself from your mission.

If there is any controversy at all regarding your relationship status; for example, if one or both of you is already in a relationship or just coming out of a relationship, be clear about your boundaries. Check with him to be sure he is comfortable with you sharing your relationship status. Make sure he is ready before being open about a relationship that could create scandal.

If he is not clear of a past relationship or marriage, it may be best for you to uphold strong boundaries so as not to attract controversy or gossip.

Keep disagreements private and definitely off of Facebook and social media. Don't get into dramatic scenes in public. Both disagreements and displays of affection are private business to a Capricorn man.

5. Breaking with His Beloved Traditions

Think twice before challenging a Capricorn man's routines and traditions. He may only see his family once each year for a holiday, but he craves all the traditions from food to music to decorations.

He loves immersing himself in cultural, religious and family traditions. It is his one break from all work and no play. It is one of the few sentimental things a Capricorn man will get drawn into. Even if he seems modern in many ways, don't make the mistake of assuming he is not a traditional guy at heart.

Aimee's story:

Aimee and Lance had been together almost a year. Coming up on their first Christmas together, this couple was faced with their first major challenge. Aimee's mother was in poor health and Aimee wanted to spend the holiday with her parents. Her nieces and nephews would be visiting from out of town and staying with her parents only for Christmas Eve, so it was important to her to try to be with her family that evening to see everyone.

Lance had family out of town and everyone always went to his parents' home for a big celebration that spanned several days and actually began the day before Christmas Eve.

No problem, Aimee assumed. They could see her family Christmas Eve and spend the rest of the time with his family, right?

Wrong.

Lance was deeply upset that she would suggest taking one day away from his tradition. Aimee couldn't believe what she was hearing and thought Lance was being totally selfish. Maybe you think that too. And maybe he was being selfish, but he was also doing exactly what Capricorn men do.

He wanted to savor every part of the family tradition and there were set things that took place every night of their gathering. He had never in all his life missed out and didn't want to start now. Plus he was additionally upset at the idea that his partner would not join him in his family's tradition.

I know what you're thinking. That's ridiculous. Why doesn't he have a heart? Her mother is ill. Why couldn't he understand?

Well, truth be told he understood just fine. The difference was not whether he understood but whether he could bring himself to break a valuable tradition from his past. This is easier said than done for a Capricorn man. It doesn't make him right or wrong - it is just his style.

Aimee assumed he was being heartless and uncaring and, of course, selfish.

Eventually they came up with a compromise but the fact that he hadn't automatically seen her point of view left a bad taste for her. She didn't enjoy their plans as much as she could have otherwise because in the back of her mind she kept thinking that he had been so selfish and unreasonable.

It wasn't until months later when she stumbled across my website and read some of the information about a Capricorn man that she reached out to relay her story. Luckily, they are still together and doing great.

Even after the fact, being able to put the pieces together and realize that her Capricorn man was not trying to be difficult but was just being, well, a Capricorn man, put Aimee's mind at ease.

Sometimes it isn't what we do but why we do it that counts. Though on the surface level his reaction seemed unreasonable and silly, understanding how much security a Capricorn man derives from the past and from his traditions can put his behavior into a different perspective.

Understanding what tradition means to a Capricorn man

He's grown. He has no kids and Aimee's mother was sick. So why was there even an argument away from spending the holidays with her family?

Because kids or not, sick parent or not, Lance's family and their traditions were still important to him. Next to a Cancer man, a Capricorn man is the most tied to family and tradition in the zodiac. Odd as it sounds, it's almost offensive to him to suggest doing something new or different.

Though he seems selfish at first, try to understand what tradition means to a Capricorn man. They are anchored not only to the past but by the past. Their family, traditions and values give them an understanding of themselves and their purpose.

A Capricorn man separated from traditions will feel like he's freefalling. He will feel completely unmoored and ungrounded. This is terrifying to him. Something that seems like a harmless change in plans or even a positive adventure will be frightening to a Capricorn man.

He doesn't like to talk about his vulnerability. Instead, he will just insist on having his way. He needs to feel the security of re-living his past which is something traditions allow him to do.

Avoid breaking any longstanding plans at short notice

If possible, stick to plans you make with a Capricorn man. If you're careless about your commitments he'll feel insecure and even anxious. Once or twice, if there is an emergency, he can be understanding.

Yet if you are chronically offering alternative plans at the last minute, you'll make a Capricorn man dizzy. When a Capricorn man makes plans he feels deeply rooted in his commitment.

Even something as trivial as having laundry day on the same day every week is a big deal to a Capricorn man. If his schedule, routines and traditions are challenged, he'll become anxious and insecure about the entire relationship.

Keep traditions alive together

When it comes to family or religious traditions, try your best to blend or compromise. He will likely have a more concrete at-tachment to his traditions than you do. Try to support his traditions and join him in his celebrations if you can.

At the same time, don't lose your own grounding and your foun-dation in your own traditions. Just because he is less flexible doesn't mean he always gets his way. Doing this will only create resentment that can hurt the relationship down the road.

If you can try to plan things together that work so that you both get to attend important cultural or religious services or spend time with family, then that is ideal. If that is not feasible, work out a schedule to trade off what holiday is spent with which family or other forms of compromise.

6. Disrespecting His Family or Not Having Family Values

Even if you don't have the best relationship with your family, it's best to show respect around a Capricorn man. As the zodiac sign associated with tradition, elders and age, he will notice how you treat the elders in your family. Be careful how you talk about his family and yours. A Capricorn will be slow to forgive if he feels you don't value family.

Cori Anne's Story:

Cori Anne barely knew her mother. She was raised between two households; her aunt's and her grandmother's. She had a decent relationship with her aunt but was very distant from her grandmother. In the times she lived at her grandmother's house growing up, life was super rigid and disciplined. Her grandmother insisted on attending church every night of the week and took Cori Anne with her.

Cori Anne didn't agree with a lot of things that went on in the church, things she would later recognize as mental and emotional abuse. She still practiced her family's religion, but came to understand that the leader of this particular church was more like a cult leader.

She also had a hard time visiting her grandmother because in her old age she had become more and more fanatic about her religious beliefs. Her political and personal beliefs had also become more zealous and less tolerant. Cori Anne had a difficult time even having conversations with her grandmother for this reason.

When she met Matthew, their relationship progressed well. They had so much in common and she was really starting to fall in love. She was ecstatic when he invited her to meet his family - a big move for a Capricorn man. Cori Ann had managed to steer clear of talk about her own family. She was self-conscious about the way she grew up and didn't feel ready to share her secrets just yet.

But when they were ready to meet his parents, he came right out and asked,

"Doesn't your family want to meet the man you're dating?"

She didn't know how to answer this exactly, so she tried to be dismissive.

"My family is pretty crazy. I don't really talk to them."

Matthew was taken aback. It didn't occur to him, as a Capricorn man with a good relationship with his parents, that not everyone was so fortunate. He made the assumption that Cori Ann was being rude or disrespectful. In his mind, all families were like his family, encouraging, supportive and stable.

With this image in mind, he judged her attitude toward her family as irresponsible or even neglectful. How could she be so callous? he wondered.

He kept his reservation to himself and they went through with their plans as usual. Cori Ann was accepted by his parents who were kind and generous.

On the drive home, he said half-jokingly, "So, I know you're anti-family, but what did you think?" Cori Ann was hurt to hear him say this. She was about to argue back but then realized he had no ground to stand on to make any assessment because she had been elusive to begin with.

She decided that if they were going to be together she would have to tell him at some point. She told him the truth about her upbringing and the difficult times she had spent at her grandmother's house. How her grandmother had become more religiously fanatic recently and how it was hard to bear.

She told him that she wasn't anti-family, but that she didn't have the most emotionally supportive family and had a strained relationship with her grandmother at best now. They discussed this further and he tried to get her to think more positively. After all, he suggested, your grandmother did raise you. She may not have been parent of the year, but she did her best, right?

Cori Ann considered this and agreed but that didn't change how difficult it was to spend time with her grandmother. Matthew and Cori Ann agreed to at least try a visit and see what happened.

They made plans and spent an afternoon visiting her grandmother. After about two hours, Cori Ann was restless to leave. Still, this was the longest she had been able to visit for in a few years.

Though this conflict didn't result in a breakup or major relationship drama, it did impact Matthew's good opinion of Cori Ann. Because he was understanding about her situation and because she was willing to compromise and spend some time with her grandmother in his presence, which turned out to take some of the edge off, it worked out.

He came to see that she had valid reasons for avoiding her family and she came to see that she could spend some amounts of time with her family and not get totally stressed out.

Don't disparage his family (or yours)

Maybe you have good reason to judge your family, or his. But be careful about when, where, how and why you do so. Try to save criticism only for when it is most needed. Let little things slide if you can.

A Capricorn man will assume that all families, no matter how tense their dynamics, are fundamental to individuality. That is because unlike other signs such as Aquarius, Scorpio, Sagittarius, Leo or Aries, who value individuality above the power of the collective, Capricorn men (similar to Libra or Virgo) are equally concerned with the importance of the group or of society.

Capricorn men feel family is the bedrock of a successful individual. He's used to ignoring small slights and petty disagreements. Even major traumas may be written off by a Capricorn man. His personality makes him prone to enduring challenges and seeing hardship as character-building.

For a Capricorn man, the links to family are important. Even if his early experiences were challenging or his parents cold or aloof, a Capricorn man will take it all in stride. He will look at his difficult experiences as a source of strength and perseverance.

Likewise, if you have had challenges with your family, ranging from neglect to trauma and everything in between, a Capricorn man won't show much sympathy. He'll wonder why you aren't grateful for the character building experiences.

You may think this makes him cold and heartless but this is not the case. A Capricorn man's ruling planet, Saturn, is associated with struggle, hardship and restriction. A Capricorn man actually does thrive on hardship and challenges, and he expects others should treat these events in a similar way.

Show your connection to family or community

I get it; not everyone has a wonderful, nurturing family. Even if a Capricorn man doesn't get it, and if he's turned off by your strained connection to your family, there are ways to reassure him.

He basically wants to see that you are grounded in a community of some kind. Perhaps your closest friends are like sisters. Maybe an important mentor is like a mother or father figure to you. If you can, show respect for elders in your family or in your community at large.

Even if traumatic family experiences have left you completely disconnected from your parents or other key family members, think of the people who are like surrogate family to you. The more you emphasize the family-like role of these people in your life, the more a Capricorn man will respect you.

Even if you have difficult family ties, try to describe your family in objective ways so that you avoid excess criticism from him. A Capricorn man will be more forgiving of a rational discussion of why you don't call your parents to check in every week as opposed to a rant about how your parents always liked your sister better.

7. Interrupting His Work

A Capricorn man may love you, but he's married to his work first and foremost. He will become annoyed if you interrupt his work. Some women try to test a man to see if he's making them a high priority.

This is never a good idea when dealing with a Capricorn man. Not only is it best to not test him about anything, but you never want to test him by cutting in on his work. Even if you think he's tinkering around in his office and not doing anything "important." To a Capricorn man, everything he does is important.

Margie's story:

Margie and Brent had been together for a little more than six months. One night, he took her out for dinner at an upscale restaurant. She expected he may propose, though she thought it was a little early in the relationship. Still, they had been getting more serious.

He couldn't stop grinning.

"Margie," he began, "I brought you here to tell you something very exciting."

She rarely saw him break his neutral facial expression, so she couldn't imagine what his news would be. As drinks were served, he leaned in closer and took both her hands.

"Margie, I have been offered the promotion I've been working toward for months."

Of course she was excited for him as well. She knew how much this promotion meant to him. He remarked as their evening ended about how his schedule was going to change for a while but reassured her not to worry.

In the coming month, Margie noticed he had less time to spend with her but they made a commitment to keep a standard date every week on the same two evenings. He kept this commitment.

Yet Margie was still insecure about his distant nature. He brushed it off, saying he was overwhelmed with his new role. She thought it would be helpful to text him a few times during the day to try to give him encouraging messages.

It completely backfired.

Though her intention was to be nurturing and encouraging, he didn't appreciate being contacted during meetings or while working on a project. She could never have anticipated his negative reaction.

He started to become more silent and distant.

So she started texting more frequently, figuring maybe he just hadn't gotten the other text messages.

Finally, after three weeks of almost no contact from him, she stopped reaching out. A week later, he invited her to dinner. He told her that things were settling down at work and that he was getting into the swing of things. He also calmly stated that he did not appreciate her texting him while he was working. That he had been on the verge of reconsidering the relationship and if she hadn't backed off, he would have done.

Leave it to a Capricorn man to be so blunt.

She hadn't realized it, but after their conversation she came to understand that to him, the "inspiring" texts felt like a constant interruption.

Why he sounds so annoyed when he answers the phone

Of course, in a perfect world, a man who is feeling annoyed by being texted too frequently will simply say, "Please don't text me during my work shift," and be done with it. A Capricorn man will try to ignore little things, though.

He doesn't like to complain. His style is to just deal with things and endure until he can't anymore. Yet if you text or call a Capricorn man and he ignores you, or if he answers the phone sounding annoyed, there is a reason.

He doesn't like being interrupted when he is busy. He will miss your good intentions and instead feel like you are bothering him.

Text once, then let him follow up

Don't second guess yourself, or him. Text him once, then let him follow up. All the things that may run through your head...maybe he didn't see it? Maybe he meant to text back but forgot to hit 'send'?

Let those worries go. Remember - he's an independent, successful adult. When he's ready to respond he will. He hasn't forgotten you. He's either busy or not in the mood to talk.

Review

Whew! That was a lot to digest. Take a breath, sister. Remember, no matter what, a Capricorn man will forgive you if he sees that you are trying to create a solid foundation. You don't have to be perfect and, yes, from time to time you're going to make mistakes. Just as he will.

The best thing you can do is to try to keep these main pointers in mind. When your intentions are good and you can communicate with him in practical matters, especially if you are able to show him how you are trying to create stability, he can be forgiving and understanding.

- **Lacking Self-Discipline** - Keep to your routines. Show self-discipline and organization. Reassure him that stability is important to you.

- **Wasting Money**- Bring out the budget and cut up the excess credit cards. You won't just be helping him; first and foremost you'll be helping yourself.

- **Being too pushy** - Don't try too hard to make him commit. Capricorn men really are among the most committed and serious men in the zodiac. He will open up when he's ready.

- **Causing a Scene or Being too Controversial** - A Capricorn man works hard to avoid controversy, so don't bring it to his doorstep. Keep a low profile and protect his reputation.

- **Breaking with His Beloved Traditions** - He's a creature of habit and is tied to traditions. Celebrate his favorite past-times with him. Don't expect him to embrace change easily.

- **Disrespecting His Family or Not Having Family Values** - Show your Capricorn man that you respect family members, even if you don't get along with them.

- **Interrupting His Work** - Don't give him work-related ultimatums and don't try to come between a Capricorn man and his work. Support his success instead.

Next Steps

Now that you know the deeper motivations and inner assumptions of a Capricorn man, you'll know exactly how to avoid the common Capricorn relationship mistakes. Most of these mistakes are completely avoidable.

At worst, if you're really not sure if you've made a mistake with a Capricorn man, look for changes in his behavior. He doesn't always show emotion and can hide when he's hurt or angry.

Look instead for patterns, such as being less affectionate or shutting down communication. You may also be able to see his disapproval on his face. If you see these signs, you can always ask him outright if something is wrong.

Avoid asking, "How are you feeling?" as this is emotional language and he is more comfortable with practical language such as, "Are you ok?" or, "Is there something on your mind you want to talk about?"

Capricorn men can be independent and hard-working. They can be patient and slow-moving in relationships, but once he's committed to you he'll want to be with you for life.

I hope this guide helped you understand him better and the mistakes to avoid in order to grow your love... faster and easier.

If you still have questions - feel free to email me at Astrologer-AnnaKovach@Gmail.com and I'll try to help ;)

Sending you love! XOXO

Anna

P.S.

And if you'd like to learn more about your Capricorn man, you can also check out some of my other books and programs...

The best place to start is https://CapricornManSecrets.com

P.P.S. If you got some good insights from this book, please share your experience with other women dating a Capricorn man - I really appreciate your support!

Printed in Great Britain
by Amazon

84839497R00031